Patterning Techniques

Doodling and patterning are wonderful ways to embellish your images to make them unique to you and really stand out! You can add doodles to a design before coloring or after. Adding doodles after coloring works best on designs colored with markers, as described below.

Before Coloring

1 Start with a blank design.

2 Add little doodles like lines, circles, and other shapes. Patterns are just simple shapes that are repeated!

3 Color the design.

T0351848

After Coloring

1 After coloring a design with markers, add details using fine-tip pens.

2 Add more details using gel pens (I used glitter gel pens here).

3 Add a final layer of detail using paint pens.

Shading

Shading is a great way to add depth and sophistication to a drawing. Even layering just one color on top of another color can be enough to indicate shading. And of course, you can combine different media to create shading. Here are two techniques to try!

Shading by Outlining

If you've never tried shading before, start with this easy outlining technique to help make your images pop! In this example, markers were used for both the base colors and the outlines, but you could also create the outlines with pens, gel pens, or colored pencils.

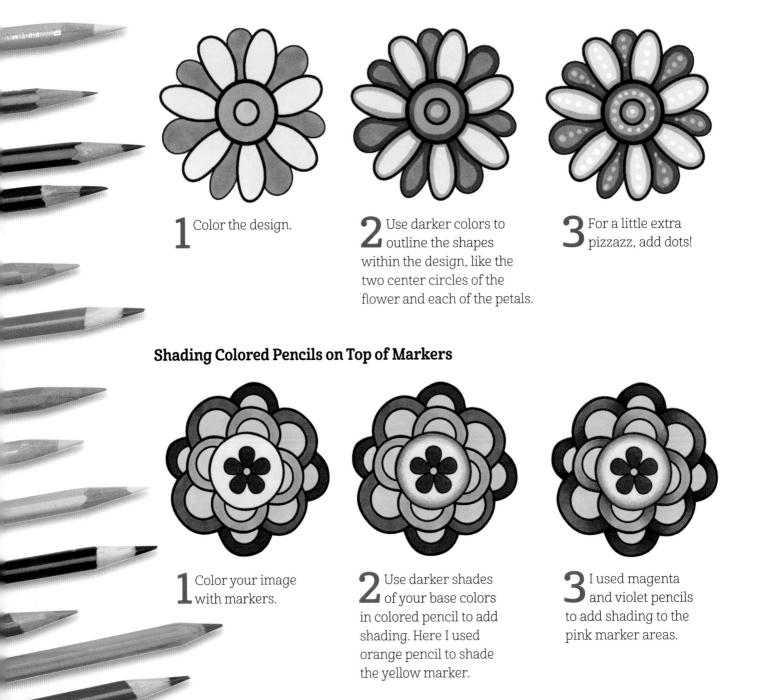

1 Color the design.

2 Use darker colors to outline the shapes within the design, like the two center circles of the flower and each of the petals.

3 For a little extra pizzazz, add dots!

Shading Colored Pencils on Top of Markers

1 Color your image with markers.

2 Use darker shades of your base colors in colored pencil to add shading. Here I used orange pencil to shade the yellow marker.

3 I used magenta and violet pencils to add shading to the pink marker areas.

Blending

Blending allows you to make smooth transitions between different tints and shades of a color when shading, and even between two different colors when creating gradients. Here are some simple techniques to produce flawless blends.

Alcohol-Based Markers

Alcohol-based markers can create smooth blends that have a painted look. You only need two colors to create a blend, but in this example I've used three shades of the same color: a light, a dark, and a color in between.

Tips

- It's easiest to create smooth transitions while your base layer is still damp.
- Don't be afraid to really work the marker into the paper—alcohol-based markers won't tear or pill the paper.
- Put a sheet or two of scrap paper underneath your coloring page to soak up any excess color that may seep through the paper.

 **1** Color your entire image with the lightest color. While this is still damp, use your middle color to add shading, focusing on the sides and bottom half of the shape.

 **2** Using your lightest color, go over the edges where the two colors meet to soften the transition.

 **3** Use your darkest color to add deeper shadows, focusing on the very outer edges and bottom of the shape.

 **4** Use your middle color to soften the edges between the dark and middle colors. If needed, use your light color on top of everything to smooth the transitions even more.

All of the colors in this flower were blended. Note the transitions from yellow to orange, from light pink to magenta, and from light blue to medium blue.

4 I used a dark blue pencil to shade the light blue marker areas. You can also use a white pencil to add details on top of the marker, as I did in the flower's center.

Tips

- When using colored pencils, apply more pressure to the areas that you want to appear darker.
- Use light-colored pencils on top of dark areas to create highlights.

Colored Pencils

In this example I've used three shades of each color:
a light, a dark, and a color in between.

1 Color the design with your lightest colors. Then, lightly apply your middle colors over the areas that you want to appear darker.

2 Lightly apply your dark colors where you want the deepest shadows. Apply more pressure where you want the color to be the strongest.

3 Use your middle colors to go over the area where the middle and dark colors overlap. Apply pressure as necessary to smooth the transitions.

4 Use your lightest colors to go over the areas where the light and middle colors overlap, applying pressure as needed.

Tips

- Applying a colored pencil in a circular motion makes the color appear more seamless than if you use back-and-forth strokes.
- Always use light pressure at first, and apply more pressure as you add more layers.
- A slightly blunt colored pencil works better for this technique than one with a super sharp point.

Colored Pencils with a Blender Pencil

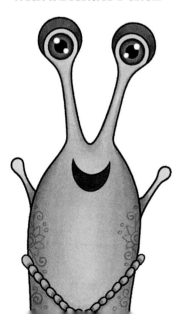

1 Lightly apply color using small overlapping circles (as opposed to back-and-forth strokes). Leave areas completely white where you would like to create highlights.

2 Using the same colored pencil and the circular motion, go back and add a second layer of color, applying more pressure to the areas that you want to appear darker.

Colored Pencils with Baby Oil

1 Color the darkest areas first.

2 Next, color in the lighter areas.

3 Dip a cotton swab or tortillon (paper blending stump) into baby oil. Blot the excess on a paper towel. Gently rub the swab over the colored areas. Use a different swab for each color group. After the baby oil has dried, you can add more color if needed and use more baby oil to blend it.

Tips

- You can apply as many colors and layers as you like before applying the baby oil.
- A little baby oil goes a long way. It helps to pour a small amount into a watercolor palette or small container.

3 Go over everything with a blender pencil, using it the same way you would use a colored pencil. The blender will smooth your colored pencil marks and increase the intensity of the color.

4 You can create additional shading using a darker color, as I've done at the end of each petal. Repeat these steps with different colors for the rest of your design.

Tips

- Practice on scrap paper to see the various results you can produce by mixing different colors.
- After you apply the blender pencil, the surface of the art will be slick, so you might not be able to apply more colored pencil on top.

Color Theory

One of the most common questions beginners ask when they're getting ready to color is "What colors should I use?" The fun thing about coloring is that there is no such thing as right or wrong. You can use whatever colors you want, wherever you want! Coloring offers a lot of freedom, allowing you to explore a whole world of possibilities.

With that said, if you're looking for a little guidance, it is helpful to understand some basic color theory. Let's look at the nifty color wheel in the shape of a flower below. Each color is labeled with a P, S, or T, which stands for Primary, Secondary, and Tertiary.

Working toward the center of the six large primary and secondary color petals, you'll see three rows of lighter colors, which are called tints. A **tint** is a color plus white. Moving in from the tints, you'll see three rows of darker colors, which are called shades. A **shade** is a color plus black. The colors on the top half of the color wheel are considered **warm** colors (red, yellow, orange), and the colors on the bottom half of the color wheel are considered **cool** colors (green, blue, purple). Colors opposite one another on the color wheel are called **complementary**, and colors that are next to each other are called **analogous**.

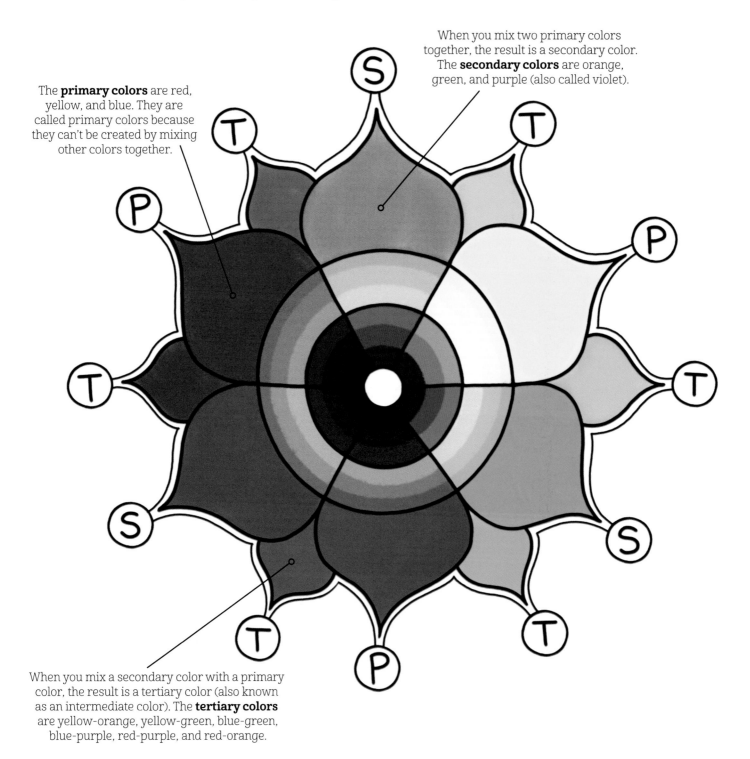

When you mix two primary colors together, the result is a secondary color. The **secondary colors** are orange, green, and purple (also called violet).

The **primary colors** are red, yellow, and blue. They are called primary colors because they can't be created by mixing other colors together.

When you mix a secondary color with a primary color, the result is a tertiary color (also known as an intermediate color). The **tertiary colors** are yellow-orange, yellow-green, blue-green, blue-purple, red-purple, and red-orange.

Color Combinations

There are so many ways to combine colors that sometimes it can be overwhelming to think of the possibilities...but it can also be a ton of fun deciding what color scheme you are going to use!

It's important to remember that there is no right or wrong way to color a piece of art, because everyone's tastes are different when it comes to color. Each of us naturally gravitates toward certain colors or color schemes, so over time, you'll learn which colors you tend to use the most (you might already have an idea!). Color theory can help you understand how colors relate to each other, and perhaps open your eyes to new color combos you might not have tried before!

Check out the butterflies below. They are colored in many different ways, using some of the color combinations mentioned in the color wheel section before. Note how each color combo affects the overall appearance and "feel" of the butterfly. As you look at these butterflies, ask yourself which ones you are most attracted to and why. Which color combinations

feel more dynamic to you? Which ones pop out and grab you? Which ones seem to blend harmoniously? Do any combinations seem rather dull to you? By asking yourself these questions, you can gain an understanding of the color schemes you prefer.

Tip

Now you're ready to start experimenting on paper. When you're getting ready to color a piece of art, test various color combos on scrap paper or in a sketchbook to get a feel for the way the colors work together. When you color, remember to also use the white of the paper as a "color." Not every portion of the art piece has to be filled in with color. Often, leaving a bit of white here and there adds some wonderful variety to the image!

Warm colors

Cool colors

Warm colors with cool accents

Cool colors with warm accents

Tints and shades of red

Tints and shades of blue

Analogous colors

Complementary colors

Split complementary colors

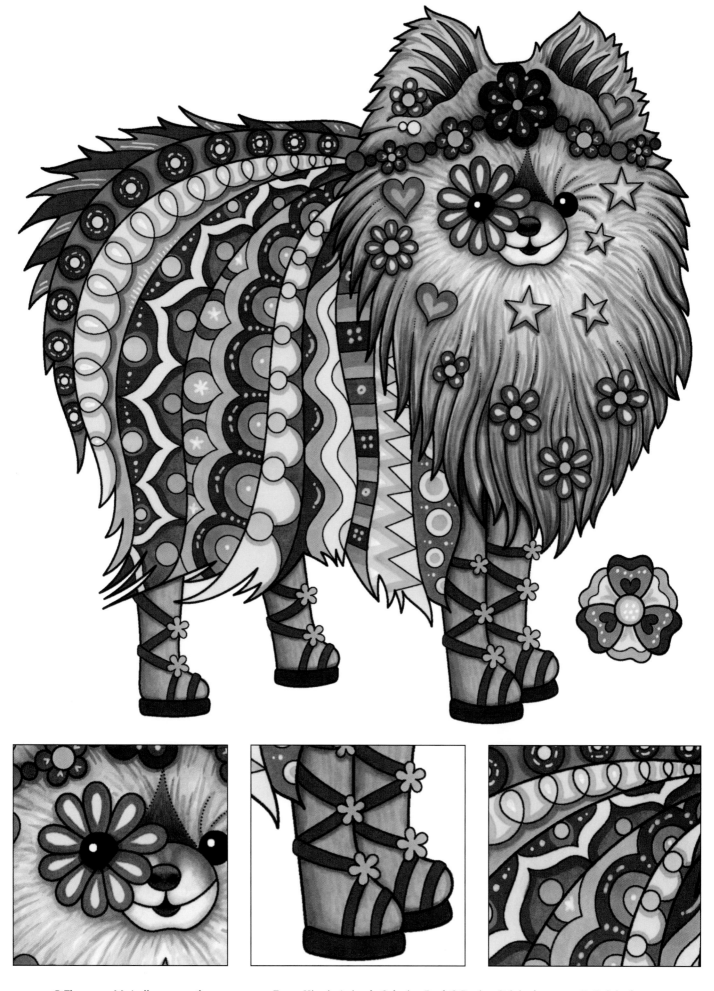

Be groovy or leave, man.

—Bob Dylan

Orang hutan is Malay for "forest person."

_____
_____
_____
_____
_____
_____
_____
_____
_____

Old hippies don't die, they just lie low until the laughter
stops and their time comes round again.

—Joseph Gallivan

A lot of birds eat twice their weight in food every day;
keep that in mind the next time you hear the phrase "to eat like a bird"!

_____
_____
_____
_____
_____
_____
_____
_____
_____
_____
_____

If there were to be a universal sound depicting peace,
I would surely vote for the purr.

—Barbara L. Diamond

A group of cats (an unusual sight!) is called a "clowder."

_____

_____

_____

_____

_____

_____

_____

_____

_____

_____

If you see that everything has spirit and that everything is connected, you honor everything because you know that it has a part to play in creation.

—Kent Nerburn, *The Wolf at Twilight*

The douc langur, which lives only in the forests of Cambodia, Vietnam, and Laos, can leap 20 feet from one branch to another.

As I go walking that freedom highway,
nobody living can make me turn back.
This land was made for you and me.

—Woody Guthrie, "This Land Is Your Land"

Raccoons like to rinse or rub their food on their fur
before eating—even the scraps they dig out of your trash can!

The smaller the creature, the bolder its spirit.

—Suzy Kassem, *Rise Up and Salute the Sun*

Rabbits beware! Whippets are one of the fastest dog breeds on Earth,
able to run as fast as 38 miles per hour.

Observe and reflect,
and become a little wiser every day.

—Doe Zantamata

While male emperor tamarins can only see two colors,
which helps them spot camouflaged predators, most females see three colors,
which makes them experts at detecting ripe fruit.

_____

_____

_____

_____

_____

_____

_____

_____

_____

The most important kind of freedom
is to be what you really are.

—Jim Morrison

Poodle comes from the German word *pudel*, which means "puddle."

With the textured look that only colored pencils can give,
you can make the body of a plain guitar look like
it is carved from spruce!

So wild animals, wild plants, wild landscapes are the healing dreams from the deep singing mind of the earth.

—Dale Pendell, *Living with Barbarians: A Few Plant Poems*

Dolphins in the wild can live longer than 40 years.

Temper the fiery attitude of this glitzy Pomeranian
with some blue and yellow flair!

You can always find hope in a dog's eyes.

—Unknown

Though they don't do much hard work these days,
Pomeranians are actually descended from sled dogs!

_____

_____

_____

_____

_____

_____

_____

_____

_____

_____

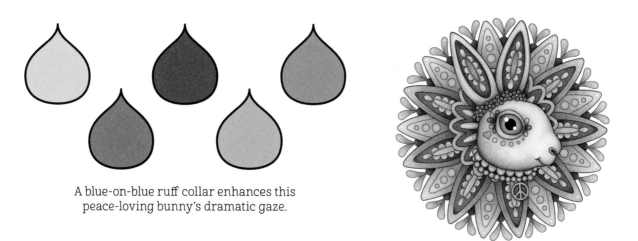

A blue-on-blue ruff collar enhances this
peace-loving bunny's dramatic gaze.

Don't hate. Meditate.

—Unknown

Like us, each and every rabbit has its own personality.

_____

_____

_____

_____

_____

_____

_____

_____

_____

_____

By using the same colors in the owl's eyes
as you use in the pattern surrounding the owl,
you'll add an interesting symmetry.

The eternal being, as it lives in us,
also lives in every animal.

—Arthur Schopenhauer

A group of owls is called a "parliament."

_____
_____
_____
_____
_____
_____
_____
_____
_____
_____

Build an analogous color palette around brown to give your snail a down-to-earth vibe—and then get creative with its shell!

Peace in my heart. Peace in my soul.
Wherever I'm going, I'm already home.

—Jason Mraz, "Living in the Moment"

The only difference between slugs and snails? Snails have shells.

Show you can dig it by making these bell bottoms
shine like rainbows in the desert.

The soul invariably travels at the speed of a camel.

—Arabic proverb

Camels have two rows of super-thick eyelashes
to protect their eyes from the desert dust.

Put this zen sloth in a good place by backgrounding with a deep, textured green—the color of harmony.

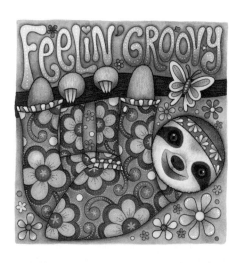

To a mind that is still, the whole universe surrenders.

—Lao Tzu

Although sloths spend most of their time in trees,
they're surprisingly excellent swimmers!

_____
_____
_____
_____
_____
_____
_____
_____
_____

This drumming sesh could last a while—better make these jeans look as soft and comfortable as possible!

Love and peace are eternal.

—John Lennon

In Egyptian mythology, Heket is a frog-headed goddess who represents fertility and childbirth.

Change is not merely necessary to life—it is life.

—Alvin Toffler

Jellyfish range in size from the width of your fingertip to eight feet across, with tentacles that can reach 200 feet long.

There is peaceful. There is wild.
I am both at the same time.

—Nayyirah Waheed

Great swimmers and excellent climbers, black panthers are actually pumas,
leopards, or jaguars with dark fur that matches their dark spots.

Like a true Nature's child,
We were born,
Born to be wild.

—Steppenwolf, "Born to Be Wild"

Lions are not shy: their roars can be heard up to 5 miles away.

It's wonderful when you can bring sparkle
into people's lives without fading away from
your own true color. Keep the hue in you.

—Dodinsky

Along with bonobos, chimpanzees are our closest living relatives on Earth.

_____

_____

_____

_____

_____

_____

_____

_____

_____

_____

Rocking to the rhythm of a groovy beat.

—Pinball, "Rocking to the Beat"

Alpacas communicate with each other by humming.

The light within me honors the light within you.

—*Namaste* translation

Only the males are actually "peacocks";
females are "peahens" and babies are "peachicks."

_____

_____

_____

_____

_____

_____

_____

_____

_____

_____

You make everything groovy, wild thing.

—Jimi Hendrix, "Wild Thing"

Pandas don't need bedrooms. When they get tired,
they just lie down on the ground wherever they are at the time.

_____
_____
_____
_____
_____
_____
_____
_____
_____

Study the nature around you, but also within you.

—Fennel Hudson, *A Meaningful Life: Fennel's Journal - No. 1*

The arctic fox likes it cold: it doesn't feel the chill
until the thermometer hits about -58°F!

Quiet the mind, and the soul will speak.

—Ma Jaya Sati Bhagavati, *The 11 Karmic Spaces*

Cows were first domesticated in southeast Turkey around 10,500 years ago.

_____

_____

_____

_____

_____

_____

_____

_____

_____

_____

We live by the sun, we feel by the moon, we love by the stars, we live in all things, all things live in us.

—Stephanie Kaza

When horses look like they're laughing,
they're actually trying to figure out whether a smell is good or bad.

_____

_____

_____

_____

_____

_____

_____

_____

_____

_____

A time for love, a time for hate,
a time for peace, I swear it's not too late.

—The Byrds, "Turn! Turn! Turn!"

Some species of snakes can see infrared, which is not a bad skill to have at night!

_____
_____
_____
_____
_____
_____
_____
_____

Don't question why she needs to be so free.
She'll tell you it's the only way to be.

—Rolling Stones, "Ruby Tuesday"

Wallabies can only hop forwards, not backwards.

_____

_____
_____
_____
_____
_____
_____
_____
_____

Life, I love you, all is groovy.

—Simon & Garfunkel, "The 59th Street Bridge Song"

Most lemur communities are dominated by females,
even though female lemurs are smaller than male lemurs.

_____
_____
_____
_____
_____
_____
_____
_____
_____
_____

Ride the energy of your own unique spirit.

—Gabrielle Roth

Pygmy marmosets live on sap and gum from trees.

_____
_____
_____
_____
_____
_____
_____
_____
_____
_____

Got to get back to the land and set my soul free.

—Crosby, Stills, Nash & Young, "Woodstock"

One way De Brazza's monkeys communicate is by shaking tree branches.

_____

_____

_____

_____

_____

_____

_____

_____

_____

_____

Your mind is like a parachute—it doesn't
work unless it's open.

—Unknown

Elephants recognize themselves in mirrors.

_____
_____
_____
_____
_____
_____
_____
_____
_____
_____
_____